Seeing COLORADO'S

FORESTS
for the TREES

Photography by JOHN FIELDER

Text by STEVE SMITH

WESTCLIFFE PUBLISHERS

westcliffepublishers.com

Burn area near Trappers Lake, White River National Forest

JOHN FIELDER

Wildfires destroyed more forest in the summer of 2002 than during any other single season in Colorado's recorded history. The 140,000-acre Hayman Fire in the South Platte River drainage of Pike National Forest was the largest fire Coloradans have ever seen. Fires in the San Juan National Forest near Durango, the White River National Forest near Trappers Lake and Glenwood Springs, and in Routt National Forest near Steamboat Springs destroyed trees, dwellings, and businesses, displacing people and wildlife alike. The culprits included three straight years of record-breaking drought, the logging of old-growth forests since the nineteenth century, and the suppression of forest fires during most of the twentieth century.

The drought could last another year or fifty. Around the year 1250, the effects of fifty years of minimal precipitation probably brought to an end the Anasazi civilization in southwest Colorado. With drought comes fire, and there's very little we humans can do about it. Some people suggest that we thin our forests by cutting down trees in order to reduce fire intensity, but this is an expensive option. Considering that trees cover 20 percent of Colorado's total area—some 13 million of our 65 million acres—there's just too much forest here for thinning to make a difference. In addition, logging requires new roads, and roads fragment wildlife habitat.

More important, shouldn't we consider whether wildfire suppression is even appropriate? Reducing the risk of fire around our homes and businesses is certainly necessary, but what about on our public lands? Shouldn't we look more closely at the role of fire in nature's ecosystems before we draw any conclusions? What is nature's way, and what processes, manmade or natural, promote healthy forests?

This book is intended to both increase your appreciation for trees and forests through photography, and help you to better understand how forests work by way of Steve Smith's discussion about forest ecology. In anticipation of an extended drought, Colorado's citizens and their elected leadership must make important decisions at both state and federal levels. We should base these decisions on sound science and an appreciation for preserving Colorado's natural heritage. It is the obligation of our generation to leave Colorado intact with the same essentials that we have enjoyed—clean air, clean water, wild places, open space, beautiful vistas, and diverse forests. Ultimately, we are morally charged with protecting a legacy that has taken 4 billion years to evolve: life on Earth.

This book's images, made during a ten-year period, represent trees and forests in all four seasons. Incidentally, spring and fall are the only times when I get to enjoy nature all by myself. Summer forays into the wilderness require "sherpas" and llamas to carry way more camera equipment and camping gear than I can shoulder on my own. Winter excursions to remote mountain huts require friends on backcountry skis to take along the wine and food while I tote the cameras.

However, when Colorado's deciduous trees leaf out in May and June and drop their foliage in September and October, I can photograph alone. Colorado's vast network of roads and highways provides easy access to prime places to photograph aspens, cottonwoods, and scrub oaks— no remote hiking required to make a gorgeous image! (By the way, pick up a copy of my travel guide, *John Fielder's Best of Colorado*, if you'd like to learn about my favorite places to photograph Colorado's trees and forests.) Comfortably cool temperatures and a scarcity of tourists lend to the joy of traveling in Colorado during spring and fall. The two weeks at the end of May produce glorious "new" greens just as sublime and photogenic as the yellows, oranges, and reds of autumn. I have not forgotten our coniferous friends: The dark greens of ponderosa and bristlecone pines, blue and Engelmann spruces, and subalpine and Douglas firs decorate these pages, too.

So what about the title of this book? You know the popular adage, "He can't see the forest for the trees." Sometimes people have a difficult time seeing the big picture, the true meaning of something, or in this case, the nature of forest ecology and what processes must always occur to ensure sustainable forests and a healthy planet. Forests do their thing during multicentury cycles, not during a human lifetime, therefore, we need to be patient and wise when it comes to forest management. It's my hope that this book will help to make understanding such things a bit easier.

DENVER, COLORADO

Seeing COLORADO'S FORESTS for the TREES

by Steve Smith

The clearest way into the Universe is through a forest wilderness.
—John Muir, *John Muir, In His Own Words: A Book of Quotations*

 ## THE FOREST MOSAIC

Among nature's more familiar creations, trees are perhaps its most amazing. In variety, adaptability, and ubiquitous distribution, trees have few faunal equals in Colorado or in the world. As a source of sustenance, shelter, and aesthetic comfort, trees take on a special beauty and value in human eyes and hands.

Forests, however, engender a complexity and an intrigue far beyond the simple sum of individual trees. Ranging from arid foothills dominated by stately ponderosa pines to ridgelines clutching tenacious, wind-sculpted bristlecone pines, Colorado's forest ecosystems shelter and feed a wild array of plants, animals, and even the very soil and flows of water so basic to terrestrial life.

Most of the tree species found in Colorado today have ancestors that flourished in the warmer climate of a flatter continent some 50 million years ago. As the Rocky Mountains rose, as remnant Ice Age glaciers alternately advanced and retreated, and even as the jet stream changed course in response, the trees and other plants developed unique adaptations and varieties suitable to higher, cooler terrain.

The lineage of Colorado's conifers reaches back even farther, to a time before flowering plants had evolved. Perhaps 350 million years ago, cones were the primary means of reproduction for trees.

With such ancestry and variety, Colorado forests now present an intricacy that is at once fascinating and almost impossible to fully understand.

Lower-Elevation Specialists

Majestic galleries of cottonwood provide shade and charm to many streamsides throughout Colorado. Standing tall from prairie to higher mountain foothills, the cottonwood species vary in size, leaf shape, and canopy, but all show off their distinctive, flickering leaves.

Prairie cottonwoods—the grandest and most familiar, with their wide leaves and large, twisted branches—dominate high-plains riparian areas along rivers such as the Platte, Arkansas, and Rio Grande. Fremont, longleaf, and lanceleaf cottonwoods occupy stream niches best suited to their characteristics. Even the distinctive aspen of higher mountain groves is a cottonwood relative.

Scattered piñon-juniper stands endure in drier hill country, generally between 4,000 and 9,000 feet in elevation. They vary greatly in size according to the amount of water they receive, and often grow in twisted shapes, sculpted by wind and slope. These trees anchor and shelter a remarkable show of wildlife, including songbirds and gregarious jays, mule deer and their predators, diverse rodents, and coyotes, in otherwise inhospitable country.

Tangled groves of Gambel oak, some 4,000 years old, cover steeper, low-elevation slopes in western parts of the state. These tough and weathered collections might well be called forests, but they typically better resemble groves or mazes. Being oaks, these small-trunked trees grow very slowly and are able to endure extreme changes in moisture availability extending over many years.

The Magic of Evergreens

It is the forest of conifers—pines, firs, and spruces (and their colorful tagalongs, aspens)—that more often comes to mind when conjuring an image of sylvan Colorado. These supremely adapted forests stay green all year, surviving, even thriving, in the extremes of weather and season. In overlapping and puzzle-pattern ecological zones, they almost universally cover the landscape between 5,500 and 10,000 feet in elevation.

Beginning with the children's lesson in distinguishing among the three primary conifers, identifying them by their needles—**f**irs are **f**lat, **s**pruces are **s**quare, and **p**ines are in **p**airs or more—there is a universe of discovery available within the forest. The basic definer of mountain landscapes, protector of water and soil, habitat for creatures of almost limitless diversity, and a place to restore and refresh the human spirit, the forest has much to tell even as it harbors some special mysteries.

The following descriptions, moving sequentially upward in elevation, begin this tour of Colorado forests by helping to orient the visitor and give the terrain a new depth of personality.

Stately Giants

Ponderosa pine trees punctuate forested land at drier and lower elevations. Actually, when found in their natural condition, gatherings of these trees barely compose a contiguous forest. Adapted to warm, dry conditions, ponderosas stand apart to conserve water and nutrients. In fact, the trees absorb so much of the available water and nutrition that few, if any, other plants grow under them. Grasses and limited shrubs make up most of the sparse understory, which is also kept in check by frequent, fast-moving, low-intensity ground fires that do not harm the large trees.

Ponderosas are Colorado's biggest conifers, often growing 150 feet high and sporting a girth of four feet in diameter. The lower trunks are typically free of branches and are covered in thick, red bark with trademark spiral splits. Sensitive to cold, ponderosas seldom venture above 7,000 feet, although they might appear in more sheltered, dry areas up to 9,000 feet.

The combination of big trees and expansive savannah found in the ponderosa forest supports a wide array of alert and generally fast-moving wildlife. Squirrels and chipmunks scamper in and among the trees, while mule deer, elk, and rabbits forage around them and take advantage of the long defensive-sight distances. The trees' split bark shelters insects that, in turn, attract adept extraction by Steller's jays, flickers, and woodpeckers.

The open mountain parkland created by the widespread ponderosa is ideal for grass foragers. The human visitor expects at any moment to see a herd of American bison grazing here as they did a century ago.

The Big Woods
The spruce-fir forest is probably the one most familiar to mountain visitors, mainly because of the wide range it covers. Also, this is the portion of the forest most frequented for recreation because of its buffered, generally temperate weather. Curiously, the densely growing forest primarily creates that subclimate on its own.

This zone is truly the heart of the Rocky Mountains. It serves as the primary source of clean, fresh water for agriculture and cities below. Its wetlands and glades add dramatically to the larger region's biological diversity, providing essential habitat for literally thousands of plant and animal species.

Ponderosa pines, blending into the zone from lower elevations, favor dry, sunny, south-facing slopes. Engelmann spruces, subalpine firs, and blue spruces tend to grow on shadier, moister, north-facing slopes.

Distinctive for its size and for the pale blue accent of its younger needles, the blue spruce stands out among its fellow spruce-fir companions. It captured the admiration of early settlers who ultimately chose it as Colorado's state tree.

More rare than ponderosa pines, spruces, and other fir species, stands of stately Douglas firs appear mixed on both north- and south-facing slopes. However, they especially tend to rise from moist, rich soils in sheltered valleys, mostly along Colorado's Front Range.

The name conifer comes from the Latin word for cone, the feature of these trees that gives them both a unique appearance and the means to multiply. Seeds form on the scales of the cones after fertilization through a colorful dusting of pollen falling from male flowers higher in the tree. The process yields clouds of yellow pollen and, sometimes with the help of squirrels, a rain of crisp, bright cones.

At first look, the spruce-fir forest appears uniform, with little diversity. Slightly deeper exploration, however, reveals a world of interconnected complexity with ever-unfolding layers of beauty and natural wonder.

These trees generally grow densely, leaving little room for sun to reach the forest floor. As a result, understory plants such as kinnikinnik, evening primrose, mountain mahogany, and the star of Colorado botany, blue columbine, are limited in size but not in variety. Wildlife includes secretive creatures such as voles, martens, and squirrels.

An outing in the spruce-fir forest is a storybook tale of time in the woods. Wildlife constantly flits and dashes; the varieties of flowers, shrubs, and trees are almost too numerous to count. Mountain breezes are bracing—sometimes gentle, sometimes hinting at the fury that can topple whole groves of the mighty evergreens. A visit here is always refreshing.

Nature's Tree Farm
Colorado's most common conifer, the lodgepole pine grows in dense stands of uniform trees. Regenerated by fire that both opens the stand and opens seed cones, these trees are often of similar age over vast areas. They are typically small in diameter, burn more readily than other evergreens, and are susceptible to the rapid spread of insect and other infestations. The thick lodgepole forest affords little space or support for wildlife or smaller vegetation, rendering a relatively barren forest floor.

Quick to invade burned or otherwise disturbed areas, lodgepole pine forests extend over a wide range of elevation, from 8,500 to 10,000 feet. Lodgepole pines often mix with other conifers, providing successional shelter for some species. Shade-loving firs and spruces take advantage of the dark forest floor created by the dense lodgepole stands and gradually replace the tall, lanky trees with greater diversity.

The lodgepole forest attracts few animals, primarily small and stealthy rodents, rabbits and hares, weasels and pine martens, squirrels and chipmunks. A general quiet rules this place.

Colorful Contrast
Curiously, a very different forest type often appears in the same disturbed areas favored by the dense, dark lodgepole pines. Quaking aspen groves bring a more open, lighter, livelier atmosphere to the forest.

Aspens grow tall and generally straight, rising toward the sun. This preference for light also causes lower, more shaded leaves and branches to die and fall away, leaving a concentration of quaking growth near the top of each tree and distinctive dark knots on the trunk below.

Connected by a single root system, aspens spread in circular patterns and grow quickly. In fact, an aspen stand is considered to be the world's largest organism, with one of the most extensive stands growing in Colorado near Kebler Pass. Able to thrive in both dry and moist conditions, these colorful, dancing groves invite an extensive variety of companion plants and wildlife. The wild rose, daisy, lupine, shrubby cinquefoil, and again, the elegant columbine, cover the aspen-grove floor. The deciduous aspens lose their leaves seasonally, contributing to more rapid soil-building and supporting a multistoried range of undergrowth. That vegetative variety, in turn, attracts foraging deer and elk, an array of small mammals more diverse than in lodgepole pine areas, and quick-flitting songbirds and woodpeckers.

More light, activity, and sound fills the aspen grove than nearby coniferous forests. A mountain visitor readily lingers in the aspen forest, a place of bright, filtered light, many colors, and a refreshing sense of active life. To stretch out on the ground and look up through flickering aspen crowns is pleasantly disorienting, setting the imagination to run freely.

Gnarled Patience

Just as the stunted and scattered piñons and junipers of lower elevations exist beyond the edge of continuous forest stands, bristlecone pines are the short, twisted, and very individual sentinels at the edge of the high tundra.

Growing only above 7,000 feet in elevation, and more typically at the extreme edge of timberline, these hardy trees are blasted by unrestrained wind and scouring snow. They root in the smallest crevices of soil and grow very slowly. Many live a thousand years—with some surviving much longer—but stand only a few feet high.

As a result, the bristlecones afford little shelter for other plants or wildlife. Twisted in flagged shapes stretching downwind and almost devoid of bark, these ancient trees accent the high mountain ridges and stoically mark the end of the forest's reach.

Surprisingly, the sparse-looking tundra teems with life, all species carefully adapted to the conditions and colors found there. The white-tailed ptarmigan changes its feathers to blend with seasonal surroundings: mottled brown and gray in summer, pure white in winter. Elk and bighorn sheep traverse these slopes during the brief and relatively lush summer. The quick-moving and sharply chirping pika works the boulder fields, setting aside rock-sheltered storehouses of grass.

Many plants here are the same as those found at lower, more sheltered elevations. To survive on exposed slopes and rolling ridges, tundra-dwelling plants grow much smaller, pressing closely to the ground.

To walk on the tundra, among the ancient bristlecones, is to feel the mountains' elements at their rawest and most exposed. The air is absolutely clean and invigorating. The sun seems much closer and more brilliant. Yet, a sharp, cold wind can prompt a shiver even on the sunniest day. The distant views of Rocky Mountain majesty encourage lingering, nonetheless.

The knowledgeable and sensitive traveler on the tundra treads carefully, avoids making any disturbance to the soil or plants, and keeps to established trails whenever possible. Damage here repairs very slowly, leaving scars that can remain for a century.

Champion Trees

To many people, every tree is a wonder. Some individual examples stand out, however, gaining special distinctions in size, age, or appearance.

The Colorado Tree Coalition maintains a registry of the state's most distinctive trees, or, at least, the biggest. Based on the explorations of botanists, professional foresters, outdoor recreationists, and backyard gardeners, the list includes what the group calls Champion Trees, the largest examples of each species found here so far.

Some samples from that list testify to the wonder and variety of Colorado forests, as well as to the reverence and enthusiasm that they engender among the people who visit them. For example, the largest blue spruce found so far in Colorado grows in the San Juan National Forest, measures 129 inches around the trunk four feet above the ground, and reaches a height of 153 feet, with a characteristically narrow canopy averaging twenty-six feet across. The largest Engelmann spruce, this one in the White River National Forest, is 135 feet tall and an incredible 146 inches

in circumference. An astounding Douglas fir boasts a girth of 202 inches and a height of 111 feet.

Perhaps the most majestic of Colorado trees, the largest prairie cottonwood in the country is found near Hygiene. Anchored on a trunk 432 inches around, it stands 105 feet tall, with a canopy that, on _average,_ is ten feet wider than the tree's height. By distinct contrast, but no less endowed with rugged majesty, a bristlecone pine high in the Pike National Forest is 166 inches around, hunkers at a brave thirty-five feet tall and twenty-nine feet across, and is probably much older than almost any other tree in several states.

The search for larger trees continues, but those already found testify to the amazing diversity and endurance of Colorado forests.

 CULTURAL FORESTS: THE WOODS AND PEOPLE

Since their earliest arrivals on this continent, humans have been deeply affected by forests and, increasingly over the centuries, have greatly affected them. The first people moved across bridges of ice and land from Asia to the North American continent and lived here for many centuries before significantly altering the landscape. Hunting, gathering, and the simplest forms of agriculture depended on the seasonal and cyclical character of natural ecosystems. Early humans found most success in open country and along accessible streams. Forest habitation was less frequent and initially less productive.

Much later, many emigrants from Europe to the American West initially viewed both the endless prairies and the dark forests they found there as sources of mystery and fear. Historians of the American West describe how that fear dynamically interacted, and still interacts, with the comfort that comes from gaining familiarity with the landscape and with appreciation and admiration for its beauty, as well as with efforts to dominate and control nature, including forests.

So it was that pioneers ventured with trepidation into the Colorado forest for the wild sense of freedom it afforded, but felt better about being there once some of that wildness was tamed a bit. So it is still that many modern residents and visitors in Colorado have readily taken brief forays into the forests for recreation and scientific study, comforted by a return to home and structure.

Similar to the ways of Colorado's native inhabitants, most settlers lived on the land as families or in small groups, with somewhat larger communities appearing on the productive plains and near water. The first enduring urban settlements in Colorado's forested country were primarily impulsive and slapdash affairs, generally associated with the rush to supposedly quick riches in the nineteenth-century mining districts. Mining towns sprouted in rough and remote places like Georgetown, Silver Plume, Central City, Breckenridge, Leadville, Ouray, and Creede. Some transformed into cities of architectural drama, even high culture, all built on the fabulous, if temporary, wealth from the mines. Leadville was, for a few nineteenth-century years, the largest city in Colorado.

As mining diminished in financial importance, population growth shifted back to the cities in the flatter, more open, lower-elevation parts of the state. As a result, during the twentieth century's early decades, forests in Colorado served primarily as sources of important human provisions such as lumber, water supply, and livestock forage.

By the 1950s, settlement patterns focused again on the mountains and forests. Thousands of Americans used the increased mobility, prosperity, and leisure time of the era to take up diversions such as hiking, horseback trips, and the newly popular sport of downhill skiing. The forests became playgrounds as well as commodity storehouses.

Especially in the last quarter of the twentieth century, people increasingly turned to the forests as home. Responding to the same factors that carried them there for recreation, along with new building techniques and flexibility in work schedules, more and more people made their homes in the forests.

Generally inexperienced with rural living, especially rural mountain living, the new forest inhabitants have struggled with often-conflicting attitudes about their surroundings. Encounters with some wildlife—birds, deer, and most small mammals—add to the charm of living in the forest. Encounters with others—bears, raccoons, and coyotes—sometimes mean damage, messes, and a new level of fear.

Human homes in the forest fragment wildlife habitat, either prompting the annoying encounters or, ironically, dispersing and diminishing the wild creatures that were part of the initial impetus to put homes there. This fracturing of the forest is especially acute when homes are spread far apart from each other. The same allure of seclusion and wildness that draws people to live in the forest also urges them to create buffered distance from other people and their homes.

Both human habitation and recreation have spurred a rapid expansion of forest roads and trails for motor vehicles. As a result, only a handful of places in all of Colorado remain more than two miles from a road in one direction or another.

The beneficial effects of roads, at least in a superficial view, are easy to recognize. Increased access makes living in the forest more convenient. More people can reach more forested places for recreation and refuge from urban life.

Ironically, the very routes that take people to their homes and hideaways are destroying the sense of solitude and much of the natural terrain. Many wildlife species need expanses of habitat larger than the segments left between the roads. With increased access deeper into the forest, motor-carried visitors heighten the frequency of accidentally and even maliciously set forest fires.

Human life in the forest is fraught with ironies and conflicts. Among those conflicts between forest living and the forest itself, the most persistent and unpredictable could very well be wildfire.

FIRES IN THE FOREST

From the earliest days of their life on earth, humans have known an instinctual fear of fire. They have also learned to use it, in a wide variety of forms, for comfort, nutrition, industry, and even amusement.

In few places has this duality of fear and usefulness played out quite the way it does in forests. Both in a human perspective and as a key part of the natural life cycle of trees, fire is a primal and primary force.

When Wildfires Hit Home

Wildfire has always been a part of forest ecology. How much of that has been purely spontaneous and natural compared to being human-caused is almost impossible to measure now, a thousand years since humans first began living continuously on the land that would become Colorado.

Some evidence exists that those early people deliberately used fire to create grazing habitat for game or even to drive and trap that game. Certainly, not all fires began from lightning strikes or other natural sources.

By the eighteenth and nineteenth centuries, corresponding to the early stages of deliberate human management of forests, Americans increasingly viewed fire from any source as a hazard and as a waste of valuable timber. Concerted efforts to avoid and to suppress wildfire in the forests had begun by 1910.

With limited technology, early fighters of forest fires relied primarily on a growing sense of fire behavior and on healthy doses of luck in heading off fire's spread. By the middle of the twentieth century, however, the use of motor vehicles on the ground and in the air, along with persuasive fire prevention promotional campaigns, had reduced the number and size of wildfire outbreaks.

Then a new fire phenomenon swept through the forests. Although perhaps less frequent than in earlier times, forest fires took on levels of intensity that seemed unnatural and that more and more often overwhelmed human efforts to fight them. By attempting to universally eliminate fire in order to save large, commercially valuable trees, forest managers had also lost what turned out to be more positive effects of fire.

By the early 1980s, students of forest ecology and those of wildfire dynamics had compared notes enough to learn that an unnatural accumulation of underbrush and fallen trees was providing extra fuel that made modern fires nearly impossible to contain. Apparently, the smaller, more frequent fires of earlier times had helped to clear the excess fuel without harming most large trees. In many cases, fire had also created openings for natural forest succession.

When huge fires raged in Yellowstone National Park in 1988, and in several Northwestern forests at about the same time, the pursuit of a "natural" forest condition was well under way. Early in that effort, however, forest ecologists and planners encountered the basic difficulty of defining naturalness. After centuries of human alteration, through both the use of fire and its suppression, few forests retained a prehuman condition.

Through tenuous agreement, forest managers, local land planners, and forest preservation advocates have generally declared that a natural Colorado forest would be less dense than it is now, both in the number of trees and in the volume of flammable debris under them. Such conditions as found around 1850, when more intensive human settlement began in the West, generally reflect the current concept of a natural forest.

By 2002, one in four Colorado residents lived in fire-prone areas, formally called the wildland-urban interface. Most of those areas exist in forests just outside large cities. Ironically, the growing popularity of building homes in the forest has both provided the motivation to suppress high-intensity forest fires as it has helped cause them.

Modern efforts to combat forest fires have nearly always focused priority on saving human structures by trying to direct the movement of fires away from those structures. Meanwhile, many forest residents have resisted the removal of trees and other vegetation that provide the sense of seclusion and wildness that drew them to live where they do. This version of preserving the landscape makes the homes much more susceptible to catching fire.

Gradually, through building codes, fuels-removal programs, and educational promotions, forestland communities have reduced some of the fire danger near homes. Residents learn to selectively cut trees and clear smaller vegetation close to buildings and to select more fire-resistant materials for use in construction.

As noted, however, the buildup of fuels has become a problem in nearly all Colorado forests. Unnaturally intense fires, even in the remote backcountry, destroy trees of all sizes and scour the forest floor of nutrients and soil-protecting plants. Damage to watersheds and water quality becomes a companion problem in burned areas.

With expanding human settlement in Colorado forests, the distinction between urban areas and backcountry grows increasingly blurred. Fires that start in one area can quickly threaten trees and homes in another.

In addition to tree-cutting near homes, foresters increasingly use fire itself to improve conditions in more remote areas. Prescribed fires, planned for times of favorable weather and forest moisture that make them easier to control, help to remove accumulations of fallen trees and other flammable materials. Finding less to burn later, wildfires in preburned areas are less intense and slower to spread. Portions of the backcountry forest so treated recover more quickly after wildfire, and fires that start there are less likely to threaten populated areas.

Colorado officials and citizens fear the destruction and loss of life that often accompany fires of any size near homes. By the end of a notorious string of Colorado forest fires in 2002, some communities began to change planning and land-use rules in attempt to keep new homes out of the forest, farther from fire danger.

Still, the lure of visiting and even living in the forest will always persist. People who choose to put down roots there might just have to accept the dangers, along with the pleasures, of life among the trees.

Fires and Life

While much attention centers on how forest fires affect human lives, ecologists have long understood the natural, and often beneficial, part that fire plays in the lives of healthy trees and forests. Certainly, every tree that burns in Colorado suffers damage and might die in the experience. The larger forest, however, is a complex system of individual organisms, and with that complexity comes strength and endurance.

All forest types have evolved responses to fire that assist in survival and even enhance the well-being of the forest. We have learned, for example, that naturally frequent, low-intensity fires help to clear fallen trees and other flammable materials from the forests. As a result, most fires in such natural conditions are less damaging, and large trees readily survive.

In several forest types, fire actually participates in the life cycle of trees. Some forests require periodic burning to reproduce and survive in a healthy condition.

Colorado's spruce and fir species can generally thrive with or without fire. Able to maintain robust stands during long periods free of burning, they are also some of the first to reseed and sprout in a burned area. The Engelmann spruce is an example of a so-called stand-replacement tree. Susceptible to complete elimination by wildfire, the spruces quickly reseed and reoccupy scorched regions.

Ponderosa pines, on the other hand, need fire to thrive and tend to decline during long periods without it. The species benefits from the frequent, low-intensity fires that reduce the volume of flammable debris at the forest understory and floor. Ponderosas actually lend a hand in promoting such fires by releasing prodigious amounts of seed each year, fostering the thick growth of small trees that both fuels and limits the smaller fires. As a result, mature ponderosas stand apart with crowns separated, cones sealed in abundant protective sap. Limbs survive only high above the ground, reducing the spread of hotter fires.

Lodgepole pine, another species that tends toward stand replacement, employs similar features that take advantage of fire along with a distinctive type of cone that responds to hotter fires. While some of the lodgepole cones release seeds each year, others high in the tree remain sealed by sap, released only under the heat of more intense fires. This combination helps to assure the trees' survival of nearly any type of fire.

In all instances, forests subjected to cycles of light burning generate a more diverse array of plant life and wildlife habitat than do forests completely cut or completely burned. Forest managers employ this lesson in the form of prescribed burns that mimic natural forest cycles.

OTHER FOREST ATTACKS…AND DEFENSES

Somewhat more subtle events in nature also affect Colorado forests. Generally natural and predictable at their root, some such effects can be magnified or minimized by human activities.

Bugs and the Forest

The life of forested lands includes many natural cycles of destruction, rejuvenation, and progression. The immediate effects of fire in the forest are instantly perceived and are often dramatic.

Equally dramatic in their effect, but often more subtle in their action, are cyclic infestations of forest-dependent insects. The pine beetle, spruce budworm, spruce bark beetle, and Ips beetle are examples of bugs that during one or more life cycles, most often the larval stage, invade Colorado conifers for food. The insects especially covet the softer layers of wood just inside the visible bark, the very place where important tree growth occurs. As a result, individual trees usually die.

Essentially, the insects exist perennially in Colorado forests, usually in numbers small enough to have little visible or widespread effect on the larger stand of trees. However, periodic changes in forest moisture and weather patterns cause the larval invasions to increase to more epidemic levels. Trees stressed by the shortage of moisture more readily succumb to the insects, helping to increase the bugs' numbers.

Left to play out, the more intense bug effects eventually diminish. As with natural fire, these generally natural insect cycles create openings in the larger forest, resulting in greater diversity and overall endurance.

Weed Invasions

Another form of forest-altering attack is perhaps the most subtle, but it is no less damaging than fires and insects. Invasive nonnative plants can compromise the health of the forest, primarily among the smaller flowering plants and ground cover.

Human activities most typically introduce noxious weeds into the forest. Livestock feed, vehicle tires, and even hiking boots pick up seeds or seed pods from one area and readily transport them to another. While the forest has adapted responses to fire and to natural insect invasions, it harbors little defense against plants that do not normally grow there and that often have no natural enemies or controls.

In some instances, these vegetative invaders are trees. Popular in landscaping, Russian olive is unfriendly to many wildlife types and eagerly crowds out more suitable natural trees. The destructive invasion of tamarisk, or salt cedar, along Colorado waterways is legendary, both in its dominating extent and in the near impossibility of removing it.

In the coniferous forests, however, weeds are most destructive in their ability to outcompete native grasses, shrubs, and flowers. In suitable conditions, the weeds spread quickly, displacing natives by reducing sunlight, taking nutrients, or absorbing water that those natural plants need.

The usual treatment for such destructive weeds in the forest has been direct assault, most often with chemicals. In recent years, however, more innovative techniques have evolved, such as organized grazing with goats willing to eat the invaders and strict controls on the weed seed content of hay and other plant materials entering the forest. These measures have helped to reduce weed spread, if not eliminate the weeds themselves.

Forest Recreation, Enjoyment, and Threat

The forests are remarkable laboratories, inspiring refuges for relaxation and contemplation, and the largest form of public playground in the world. Held in common and available to the general citizenry, the national forests are unique among lands anywhere.

Since 1960, management of Colorado's national forests—indeed, of all federal forests—has included increasing recognition of the value of those lands for recreation. In addition to providing wood products and forage and protecting watersheds, forest managers have expanded campgrounds, road and trail networks, and interpretative displays and publications, all in response to growing numbers of forest visitors.

Recognizing such resources and opportunities, Americans flock to the forests for hunting, fishing, hiking, camping, photography, wildlife watching and study, skiing, boating, driving, and climbing. The range of outdoor activities that people might pursue, especially in public forests, is limited only by the imagination. As a result, forest managers are increasingly obliged to put limits on those recreational endeavors, or at least on the numbers of people who try to engage in them in particular places and at particular times.

For all its healthful aspects, human recreation can, and frequently does, conflict with the basic needs of wildlife, the purity of watersheds, the production of forest goods, and the quality of the recreational experience itself. The extra speed, range, and noise of motorized recreational vehicles, in particular, magnify such conflicts in the forests. With rapidly increasing frequency, citizens and managers have sought constraints on vehicles, routes, and locations used in this modern version of outdoor play.

 ## THE CHAINSAW BUZZ

For all their diversity and multiplicity of uses, forests are most often seen as a source of wood and fiber—a place to cut trees. In Colorado, however, timber cutting has recently diminished to become a relatively minor industry.

Colorado timber cutting, at least in significant volume, never fueled an industry as viable as in other forested parts of the country. This lack of major industry development resulted, in part, from the early loss of big trees to mining timbers, bridge trestles, and railroad ties. Also, Colorado trees have always been smaller than those in America's Northwest, South, and Upper Midwest, rendering them more suitable for production of small-dimension lumber and wood chips than for larger products.

The escalating interest in forest recreation helped to prompt the further decline of what little existed of Colorado's timber-cutting industry. Since about 1970,

Colorado residents have taken to outdoor recreation in increasing numbers. In short order, that interest turned into promotion, attracting visitors from throughout the world seeking the abundant playgrounds afforded by the state's large percentage of federal public lands. Most of those public playgrounds are forests, and those who play there tend to prefer a natural setting unaltered by the effects of timber cutting.

Today, three-quarters of the nation's commercial forests are privately owned, and only some 15 percent of commercial timber comes from public land. As a result, national forests in general, and Colorado's thinner forests in particular, do not have timber production as their primary function.

Nonetheless, building on traditions that date back 150 years, the timber industry continues to press for logging on national forest lands.

Cutting the Forests to Save Them

Curiously, the phenomena of fire and insects, initial forms of destruction for forests, are now often offered as justification for increased timber cutting. Cutting trees, the arguments go, will reduce forest density and susceptibility to fire; cutting trees will reduce the food source for approaching insect attacks, helping to slow their expansion. While such arguments carry some degree of accuracy, many conservationists consistently question the extent to which large-volume timber cutting should be based on them.

Other arguments, perhaps more convincing in their detail, are also presented for a comprehensive approach to fire. This approach includes some selective forest thinning, especially close to homes and communities; increased use of low-intensity, prescribed burning in more remote parts of the forests; expanded emphasis on fire prevention through the use of more suitable building materials, land-use decisions that limit housing construction in forests, and increased education about both the natural role of fire in forests and about ways to avoid its dangers; and, in a larger sense, acceptance of the fact that forests will burn, whatever else humans might try to do in response.

Similarly, a better understanding of the natural role of forest insects and concentration on controlling their effects only in priority areas might result in a generally more healthy forest.

Logging for Water

Another justification sometimes put forth by logging advocates in Colorado is the concept of increasing water yield from forested land by cutting trees. Under this theory, extensively tested in experimental forests, snow that is not trapped in tree branches or shaded on the ground will melt more quickly in spring. The runoff then travels more readily to population centers at lower elevations, where human needs for water abound.

Measurable differences have been found downstream from these experimental cuttings, but only during the wettest weeks of years of heavy snowfall, or rain, or both—never during drought years, when additional water would be useful. To take significant advantage of increased water runoff, nearly half of the forest to be treated

must be cut. Such dramatic cutting noticeably alters the landscape and can increase soil erosion.

For these reasons, forest conservation advocates and many forest ecologists have advised a very slow and cautious approach to the concept of logging for water. Often joined by defenders of wildlife habitat, recreation enthusiasts, and tourism promoters, the conservationists challenge forest management plans that include extensive clearcut logging in Colorado.

FORESTS FOREVER

The opportunity for citizens to influence such planning processes arises from a long and colorful history of public forest policy in America. In fact, the very word "conservationist" has, almost since the founding of the first colonies, carried two competing definitions and two competing camps of forest advocates. One group would conserve forests in order to ensure a steady supply of wood. The other would conserve forests for their own sake, as sanctuaries of the natural world.

From the first day that Europeans landed on what would become continental America, forests have been altered and consumed. Settlers cut trees to clear land for crops, as well as to use for fuel, shelter, and defenses.

Soon, the rich variety and density of American forests attracted other interests. From the first logging of tall, straight masts for the British navy in the early eighteenth century to felling trees for nearly every human device and structure to clearcutting forests for the manufacture of paper, industry-minded Americans cut trees as if they would never run out.

With each stage of movement westward, settlers and commercial operations tore through the country's forests, first through the white pines of the Upper Midwest, then leapfrogging to the huge firs and spruces of the Northwest, and finally turning their attention to the Rocky Mountains. Drawn to the area now known as Colorado, initially for furs in the early nineteenth century and later to mine precious metals, people cut trees with abandon. Although smaller in size and density than those in New England's Great North Woods or in the Northwest, Colorado forests rendered timbers for mines; ties and trestles for railroads; lumber for quickly sprouting buildings; and fuel to burn for virtually every human activity.

Western exploration and expansion exploded after the Civil War, accelerating everything, including the removal of the forests. By 1890, the cutting in Colorado had left slopes around Leadville, Georgetown, Cripple Creek, and other mining boomtowns bare of virtually all vegetation. Besides facing a shortage of fuel and building materials, miners and the towns that supported them faced increased flooding and mudslides that fouled the mine works, damaged buildings, and took lives.

Such destruction and shortages in a young Western state might not have been of great concern to the Eastern-based federal government and power centers in the late nineteenth century, but a new forest conservation movement was about to sweep Colorado and its neighbors into a new era of protective zeal.

Forests and Conservation

From the early years of colonial America, a handful of conservationists spoke of the need to protect forests from destruction, if for no other reason than to safeguard supplies of wood. By the 1890s, with the notion of forest devastation for private profit becoming increasingly well-known and unpopular, the conservationists' message was catching on in Washington, D.C.

In 1800, President John Adams created an Eastern Seaboard forest reserve to supply lumber and tall masts for building the new nation's Navy. Subsequent presidents set aside other reserves in 1818, 1820, and 1827.

Before that time, the federal government maintained a basic land policy of transferring public lands, or the resources on them, into private ownership as quickly as possible. By 1900, half of the nation's billion acres of timber had been cut, with four-fifths of that land transferred to private ownership.

By the turn of the last century, the government had established several important reserves primarily to protect unique natural beauty in places such as Hot Springs, Arkansas, Yosemite Valley in California, and the world's first national park at Yellowstone. While such actions represented a small shift in the government's conservation policies, the general emphasis remained on commodity production and support of private industry. In fact, the government's first actions to protect forests had their root in the maintenance of commercial supplies of timber and fiber.

News of great fires that diminished the timber supply magnified Americans' needs for wood in everyday life and their concern over the loss of forests to exploitation. In the most extensive forest fire in U.S. history, nearly 2 million acres of forest burned and about 1,500 people died near Peshtigo, Wisconsin, in October 1871. The cry for an end to forest fires and forest profiteering grew in volume.

In 1891, a rider to a general law revising federal land policies lent the president the authority to "set apart and reserve" forests. Known conversationally as the Forest Reserve Act, the legislation was intended as a defense against the prolific, and often illegal, tree cutting taking place on public lands. The law was a move to reduce the unsustainable loss of wood for building, paper, and energy supplies.

The taking of timber from public lands before that time had faced little regulation or consistency in procedure. Even the new law did not specify much about the purpose of the new forest reserves or about how they would be managed, but it did set in motion some decisive presidential actions.

President Benjamin Harrison almost immediately set aside 13 million acres of land in fifteen forest reserves, including 1.2 million acres as the White River Plateau Timberland Reserve in northern Colorado, the nation's second forest reserve and one of five established in the state within the subsequent two years. The other initial reserves were declared at Pikes Peak, Plum Creek, South Platte, and Battlement Mesa.

By February 1897, the nation's reserves totaled 17.5 million acres, and President Grover Cleveland added another thirteen reserves of 21 million acres just ten days

before leaving office early that year. Ultimately, Colorado gained nineteen forest reserves before their names and management changed in the early years of the next century.

Although quick to create the new forest reserves, the nineteenth-century presidents were unable to do much about the way the forests were treated. Financial interest in rapidly exploiting the forests was entrenched, controlled by men influential in both business and government. Moreover, the Forest Reserve Act gave no real definition or purpose to the reserves, let alone the authority and resources for controlling their use.

Congress soon recognized those shortcomings, and members introduced more than two dozen bills to correct them, finally passing the Forest Management Act in 1897. The act authorized logging on the reserves supervised by federal authority, with trees sold by the government at or above appraised value. It also delineated two specific purposes for the reserves: "…securing favorable conditions of water flows and to furnish a continuous supply of timber for the use and necessities of the citizens of the United States." Those two founding purposes would survive with little change for more than sixty years.

The new reserves were managed by the Department of the Interior's General Land Office, a tiny, underfunded agency generally perceived as corrupted by the influence of big timber companies. Ironically, the government's real expertise in the science of forestry was maintained in the Department of Agriculture's Bureau of Forestry. Led by chief forester Gifford Pinchot, the agency held authority over virtually no forestland.

President William McKinley appointed Pinchot to the post in 1898. Pinchot quickly became a roving advocate for better forest management and for putting all forest authority in the Department of Agriculture. The emphasis on management and sustained yield from forests, as contemplated by Congress and as advocated by Pinchot, stirred opposition, especially in Western states such as Colorado. Large timber magnates joined independent-minded homesteaders and ranchers in resisting any federal control on the use of natural resources in the West.

In the early years of the twentieth century, however, Pinchot and his supporters had begun to prevail, due in part to solid support from the White House. By that time, Pinchot was working for President Theodore Roosevelt, who set forth his conservationist approach in his first State of the Union address, delivered in December 1901: "The fundamental idea of forestry is the perpetuation of forests by use." He also explained, "The forest reserves should be enlarged and set apart forever, for the use and benefit of our people as a whole, and not sacrificed to the shortsighted greed of a few." Earlier that year, Roosevelt had hunted in Colorado's White River reserve, an experience that helped reinforce his commitment to forest conservation.

As chief forester, Pinchot persuaded Congress in 1905 to approve legislation that strengthened control of the forests. The law transformed the Bureau of Forestry into the United States Forest Service and granted that new agency authority over the 86 million acres of forest reserves.

In 1907, Congress acted again by renaming the reserves "national forests," further defining their management and declaring that large additions to the national forests must be made by Congress, not by the president. Hours before the law took effect, Roosevelt added 16 million more acres to the system by proclamation.

Colorado now has ten national forests (administered as six), covering a total of 13.7 million acres, about 7 percent of the national forest system. The Arapaho and Roosevelt, Grand Mesa–Uncompahgre–Gunnison, Pike and San Isabel, Routt, San Juan, and White River National Forests include most of the state's timbered land.

Management principles for the national forests, at least any mandated by Congress, changed little until 1960, when lawmakers approved the Multiple-Use Sustained-Yield Act. In addition to affirming the basic notions of maintaining a reliable supply of timber and water from national forests, the new law declared that the forests have other purposes, as well. Now the land was also to be managed for outdoor recreation, wildlife and fish resources, and livestock forage (although the forest reserves had been used for grazing from their beginning). The act also declared that preservation of wilderness and pursuit of mining are both compatible with the newly coined phrase "multiple-use."

The National Forest Management Act, approved in 1976, added requirements for involving citizens in national forest management decisions. It also prompted a comprehensive review of the national forests' roadless lands to determine their suitability for permanent protection as wilderness.

Wilderness and the Forests

Advocates of conservation have long differed on exactly how to define and implement that concept,

dividing essentially into two schools of thought. The notion of conserving natural resources for continuing consumption generally prevailed in federal policy through the first half of the twentieth century, and it still enjoys strong favor in forest management. A competing view of conservation—preservation of natural places for their own sake, free from the effects of the axe, dam, or drill—has also long endured in America.

In the 1880s and 1890s, while Gifford Pinchot pressed his agenda of forest conservation for sustained use, eloquent leaders and writers such as John Muir and Charles Sargent spoke for the forests themselves. Muir was instrumental in the 1890 preservation of additional lands near Yosemite Valley and in California's giant redwood forests. Soon, he and his fledgling Sierra Club advocated for more sweeping national policies to protect more such places.

The two views have traded victories and even have shared common supporters. In 1919, for example, young U.S. Forest Service employee Arthur Carhart was assigned to do survey work in Colorado's White River National Forest. He was to

lay out tracts of federal land around Trappers Lake for private cabin sites. Carhart quickly became enamored of the lake and the nearby Flat Tops country, a rolling prairie of tundra and lakes floating above thick forests. He persuaded his supervisor to eliminate cabin sites from the lake's margins, instead providing a campground and preserving the natural condition of the nearby wilderness.

Carhart's success in securing wilderness protection for Trappers Lake helped to launch a new effort by the preservation camp of conservationists, a push to create a national system of permanently protected wilderness areas. Carhart joined fellow forest service employees Aldo Leopold, working in New Mexico, and Bob Marshall, working in Montana, along with citizen supporters of wildland protection, in promoting the wilderness idea and eventually translating it into law.

In 1964, Congress approved the Wilderness Act, creating the National Wilderness Preservation System and designating the first official American wilderness areas. Those initial designations included 719,150 acres in five Colorado components of the system. Eleven years later, Congress added two more Colorado areas: Weminuche, still Colorado's largest wilderness at 488,200 acres; and Carhart's Flat Tops Wilderness, the state's second largest at 235,035 acres. Colorado now boasts forty-one designated wilderness areas, protecting more than 3.3 million acres of pristine country, the majority of that land in national forests.

A Vision for Truly Healthy Forests

Colorado forests enjoy widespread popularity and support as public treasures. Whether for timber production, ski outings, or ecological understanding, people interested in the forests nearly universally express their desire that forests remain healthy and available.

The same forest enthusiasts, however, often contemplate differing versions of just what characterizes a healthy forest. Increasingly, even such diverse interests have found a level of agreement in the notion that forest uses should be sustainable, that is, they should not destroy the forest in the name of using it.

An outline that might prove successful in achieving those goals of health, sustainability, and availability follows. Some ideas included emphasize smart personal actions and habits. Others are based in decisions made by the larger community. All are important steps toward protecting and maintaining the vibrant life and refreshment that sound forests afford.

The first step in protecting a healthy Colorado forest is to understand it. This knowledge, of course, is something that native inhabitants, explorers, and scientists have pursued since the first humans crossed the Bering Land Bridge 35,000 years ago. The dramatic increase in Colorado's population during the past hundred years has brought with it many means of altering the forest landscape, technology that expands faster than our comprehension of its effects.

While our knowledge is certainly based in traditional forest-related sciences such as silviculture, botany, hydrology, and climatology, the most effective insights are those gained by everyday citizens as they read about, discuss, and experience the forest firsthand.

Sometimes described as "a sense of where you are," sensitivity to the land and life around us has long served as a tool of survival. More recently, it has become an approach to enjoying the beauty of nature, and it now is a key factor in protecting that beauty.

With an improved understanding of the forest, more and more people now recognize that protecting ecological health and durability, for its own sake, is a good thing. Safeguarding the woodlands obviously benefits forest ecosystems, but it also includes human gain.

Whether viewing the forest as a source of clean water and useful wood products, as a beloved place for recreation, or even as home, we readily realize that forest health forms the foundation for our own health and security. We can see that managing the forest on its own terms might be the best way to support life on ours.

National forest management plans typically provide the most visible, and perhaps the most effective, outlines for decisions about the future of forests. As a result, citizens engage in the preparation of those plans with vigor and strong opinions. Often those opinions conflict sharply, especially on the question of immediate and unrestrained use of forest resources versus a more sustainable approach. Nonetheless, widespread citizen participation is essential to good forest management and protection.

Effective forest defenders do not need to be trained scientists or polished orators. They need only to speak up for treating the forest in a way that works today and that will continue to work for many decades to come.

Such treatment can mean that some timber will be cut, but not that timber cutting is the primary purpose of the forest. It might mean that portions of the forest remain open to responsible motorized use, but that even more of the forest will be protected from it. It might mean that the welfare of wildlife, especially that of endangered animals, will serve as a primary guide for decisions about forest use. It might mean that oil and gas can be removed from the forest to support modern human life, but that it will be extracted with caution, employing sensitive techniques that leave the forest undamaged. In general, it might mean that we use the forest less frequently and extract its resources more slowly, allowing us to closely monitor the effects of our actions and to give the forest time to recover before we take more from it.

Through our daily personal decisions and actions, both in the forest and well beyond it, we can help to keep the land of trees standing and healthy. We can exercise a sense of restraint when visiting the woods, choosing our routes and activities

carefully to lessen the damage. We can accept the idea of limits on the places we can visit and on ways in which we visit them in order to minimize our effects on nature's cycles and on wildland beauty. We can choose wood products at home, by type and by amount, that do not stress the forest's ability to supply them. We can select more efficient vehicles and appliances, helping to reduce the push to extract oil and gas and other energy sources from forests, or from any land, for that matter.

Understanding and living with forest wildfire must increasingly become the responsibility of all people in Colorado. Forests will sometimes burn, and that burning might actually enhance the health of the woods. We can make those facts less threatening by being smart about how we live in and with forests.

We can build our homes away from forested areas, clustering houses closer together to preserve more undisturbed landscape with fewer roads and fewer structures in the forest. We can make use of building materials that resist burning. We can keep flammable vegetation trimmed away from houses to help insulate them from fires. We can insist on local laws and community standards that implement these good practices everywhere.

Few reaches of Colorado's forests remain unaltered by human activity and devices. One of our priority missions can be to keep these rare samples of the wild world intact. We can support permanent protections for wilderness areas, insist that roadless areas remain so, and ensure that unique natural wonders are preserved to exist as they are.

Some of these protections will come through law and public policy, and citizens who feel comfortable in those arenas can speak up for forest-healthy decisions. Just as important, however, others can perpetuate a common respect for the wild forests through conversations with friends, family, and associates, and through setting examples for respecting those special places. This personal message can be as simple as telling a good story about a particularly enjoyable day in the woods. It can be as easy as volunteering for a day of forest cleanup or restoration projects.

Colorado is blessed with an almost indescribable treasure in its forests. The trees, streams, wild animals, marvelously adapted plants, and unparalleled vistas found here have lasted for millennia, and it is easy to assume that they will continue—whatever we do, or fail to do.

However, we are too many and too mobile to be passive about our forested wonders. We can easily lose them if we sit idly by or pretend that they will protect themselves. We must act, in small steps or in grand strides, to guarantee that the places we enjoy, the forests that serve so well to refresh us, shall endure.

OPPORTUNITIES TO HELP KEEP FORESTS HEALTHY AND BEAUTIFUL

Many organizations in Colorado guide the work of citizens who want to visit, enjoy, and protect the natural wonder of our state's forests. A few of these groups are listed in this section. All will welcome your help as a volunteer or as a contributor.

Various local groups not listed here work on projects close to home, helping people to enjoy the forests, to speak up in their defense, and to reduce fire danger near homes and communities. Opportunities to contribute to all these organizations range from small tasks to lifelong commitments—something for anyone who appreciates Colorado's enchanting forests.

• **Audubon Society** publishes guides to forest plants and animals, leads outings, and promotes forest ecosystem protection. *audubon.org/states/co; (303) 415-0130 (state office)*

• **Colorado Environmental Coalition** coordinates a variety of environmental advocacy efforts, including protection of forests and wilderness. *ourcolorado.org; (303) 534-7066*

• **Colorado Mountain Club** has led adventures, both simple and challenging, to Colorado's high country for more than forty years. Now the club has also become a strong advocate in the protection of the forests its members love to visit. *cmc.org/cmc; (303) 279-3080 (state office)*

• **Colorado Tree Coalition** maintains a registry of Colorado's biggest trees in more than 200 varieties. The group accepts nominations for Champion Trees from any citizen and promotes planting and appreciation of trees and forests. *coloradotrees.org; (970) 491-6303*

• **Colorado Wild** closely monitors timber-cutting proposals and other management plans prepared by federal agencies administering Colorado's forests, then rallies citizen comments on those plans to promote ecosystem preservation. *coloradowild.org; (970) 385-9833*

• **Colorado Wilderness Network** (based at the Colorado Environmental Coalition) is a gathering of organizations and individual citizens that collects information on potential wilderness lands and speaks up for their permanent protection. *cowildernessnetwork.org; (970) 385-8509 (Durango CEC office)*

• **Sierra Club** has, for more than a century, guided backcountry outings to help citizens understand, enjoy, and then defend wild forests and other wonders of nature. *rmc.sierraclub.org; (303) 861-8819*

• **Southern Rockies Ecosystem Project** is meticulously mapping the remaining roadless lands in Colorado's south-central mountains, in hope of preserving large expanses of wild habitat and enduring forests. *csf.colorado.edu/srep; (303) 258-0433*

• **The Wilderness Society** was founded by the first promoters of the wilderness idea, and it continues as a strong voice for wild places. *wilderness.org; (303) 650-5818*

• **Volunteers for Outdoor Colorado** orchestrates projects and provides tools and training for everyday citizens who want to restore trails, parks, public spaces, and forest-recreation opportunities. *voc.org; (303) 715-1010*

• **Trout Unlimited** helps beginning and experienced anglers enjoy fishing in Colorado, especially in the stream-rich woodlands. The group defends the quality of the state's rivers and creeks and supports public access to them. *tu.org; (800) 834-2419*

• **Western Colorado Congress** promotes volunteer action among citizens to protect natural places, including the forests of Colorado's Western Slope. *wccongress.org; (970) 249-1978*

SOURCES

Arno, Stephen F., and Steven Allison-Bunnell. *Flames in Our Forest: Disaster or Renewal?* Washington, D.C.: Island Press, 2002.

Baron, Jill S., ed. *Rocky Mountain Futures: An Ecological Perspective.* Washington, D.C.: Island Press, 2002.

Browning, Peter, ed. *John Muir, In His Own Words: A Book of Quotations.* Lafayette, Calif.: Great West Books, 1988.

Carhart, Arthur H. *The National Forests.* New York: Alfred A. Knopf, 1959.

———. *Timber in Your Life.* Philadelphia: Lippincott, 1955.

Clarke, Jeanne N., and Daniel McCool. *Staking Out the Terrain: Power Differentials Among Natural Resource Management Agencies.* Albany: State University of New York Press, 1985.

Coggins, George C., and Charles F. Wilkinson. *Federal Public Land and Resources Law.* Mineola, N.Y.: Foundation Press, 1981.

Davis, Richard C., ed. *Encyclopedia of American Forest and Conservation History.* New York: Macmillan; London, Collier Macmillan, 1983.

Fielder, John. *A Colorado Autumn.* Englewood, Colo.: Westcliffe Publishers, 1994.

———. *John Fielder's Best of Colorado.* Englewood, Colo.: Westcliffe Publishers, 2002.

Frank, Bernard. *Our National Forests.* Norman: University of Oklahoma Press, 1955.

Frome, Michael. *Whose Woods These Are: The Story of the National Forests.* Garden City, N.Y.: Doubleday, 1962.

Gates, Paul W. *History of Public Land Law Development.* Written for the Public Land Law Review Commission. Washington, D.C.: Government Printing Office, 1968.

Limerick, Patricia Nelson. *Something in the Soil: Legacies and Reckonings in the New West.* New York: W.W. Norton, 2000.

Lukas, J. Anthony. *Big Trouble: A Murder in a Small Western Town Sets Off a Struggle for the Soul of America.* New York: Simon & Schuster, 1997.

McCarthy, G. Michael. *Hour of Trial: The Conservation Conflict in Colorado and the West, 1891–1907.* Norman: University of Oklahoma Press, 1977.

Mutel, Cornelia Fleischer, and John C. Emerick. *From Grassland to Glacier: The Natural History of Colorado.* Boulder, Colo.: Johnson Books, 1984.

Nash, Roderick. *Wilderness and the American Mind.* New Haven: Yale University Press, 1967.

Whitney, Stephen. *Western Forests.* New York: Alfred A. Knopf, 1985.

Zwinger, Ann. *Beyond the Aspen Grove.* New York: Random House, 1970.

Burn area along the White River, White River National Forest

Ponderosa pines, Castle Pines, Douglas County

Old cabin along the Cache la Poudre River, Larimer County

following page: Autumn, Horse Ranch Park, Gunnison National Forest

Gambel oaks in spring, Castle Pines, Douglas County

This is the forest primeval. The murmuring pines and the hemlocks. . .stand like druids of old.
—Henry Wadsworth Longfellow

BRISTLECONE PINE FOREST, WINDY RIDGE, PIKE NATIONAL FOREST

Along the Elk River, Routt National Forest

At the gates of the forest, the surprised man of the world is forced to leave his city estimates of great and small, wise and foolish. The knapsack of custom falls off his back.
—Ralph Waldo Emerson

SPRING GREENS ALONG DIVIDE ROAD, UNCOMPAHGRE NATIONAL FOREST

Evergreens damaged by fire, White River National Forest

ASPENS AND WILLOWS ALONG THE CACHE LA POUDRE RIVER, LARIMER COUNTY

Within his somber realm of leafless trees
The russet year inhaled the dreamy air;
Like some tanned reaper in his hour of ease,
When all the fields are lying brown and bare.
—Thomas Buchanan Read

Cottonwoods at sunset below the Sneffels Range, Ouray County

Subalpine spruce-fir forest, Weminuche Wilderness

following page: Corn lilies and aspens in spring, Kebler Pass, Gunnison National Forest

A tree is a nobler object than a prince in his coronation robes.
—Alexander Pope

NEWLY LEAFED ASPENS ALONG DIVIDE ROAD, UNCOMPAHGRE NATIONAL FOREST

Autumn aspens along Divide Road, Uncompahgre National Forest

Oh steadfast trees that know
Rain, hail, and sleet, and snow,
And all the winds that blow;
  But when spring comes, can then
  So freshly bud again
Forgetful of the wrong!
        —Robert Kelley Weeks

WINTER COTTONWOODS ALONG THE UNCOMPAHGRE RIVER, OURAY COUNTY

Spring cottonwoods along the Highline Canal, Arapahoe County

JUNIPER ABOVE THE DOLORES RIVER, DOLORES RIVER CANYON WILDERNESS STUDY AREA

I love thee nature with a boundless love
The calm of earth, the storms of roaring woods
The winds breathe happiness where e'er I rove
Theres lifes own music in the swelling floods.
—John Clare

MIDDLE THOMPSON CREEK, WHITE RIVER NATIONAL FOREST

Holy Mother Earth, the trees and all nature, are witness of your thoughts and deeds.
—Winnebago saying

ASPENS AT SUNSET ALONG KEBLER PASS, GUNNISON NATIONAL FOREST

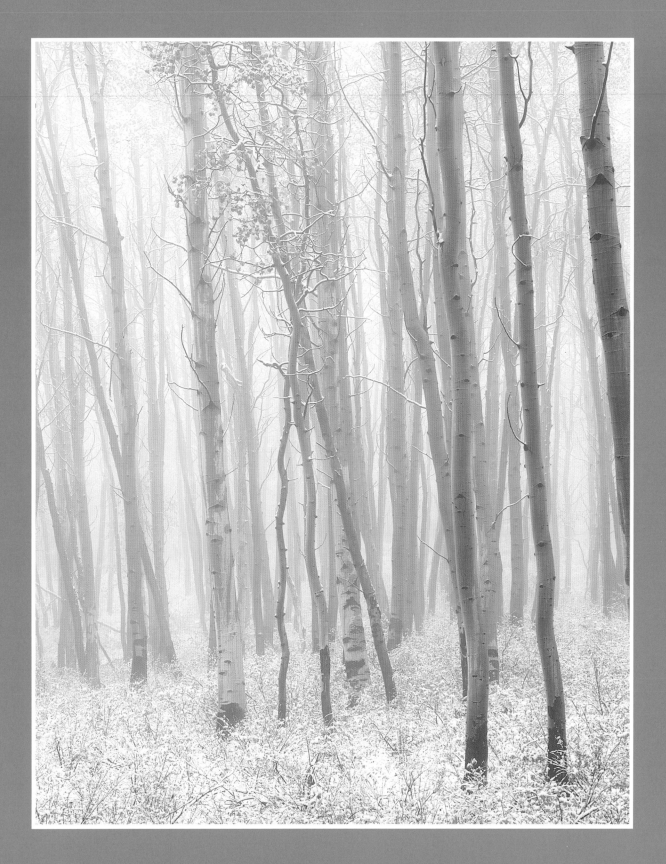

Spring snowstorm, Gunnison National Forest

Spring aspens at Horse Ranch Park, Gunnison National Forest

Sunshine is delicious, rain is refreshing, wind braces us up, snow is exhilarating;
there's really no such thing as bad weather, only different kinds of good weather.
—John Ruskin

Autumn snow, East Dallas Creek, Uncompahgre National Forest

Spruce tree in the aspens, Ohio Pass Road, Gunnison National Forest

Aspens and oaks on Dallas Divide below the Sneffels Range, Ouray County

following page: Subalpine spruce-fir forest, Sangre de Cristo Range, San Isabel National Forest

Spring aspens near Crooked Creek Pass, White River National Forest

Without enough wilderness America will change. Democracy, with its myriad personalities and increasing sophistication, must be fibered and vitalized by the regular contact with outdoor growths—animals, trees, sun warmth, and free skies—or it will dwindle and pale.
—Walt Whitman

Spring aspen reflection, White River National Forest

Aspens and conifers, White River National Forest

RUBY RANGE, GUNNISON NATIONAL FOREST

*With the din
Smitten, the precipices rang aloud;
The leafless trees and every icy crag
Tinkled like iron; while far-distant hills
Into the tumult sent an alien sound
Of melancholy.*

—William Wordsworth

How bravely autumn paints upon the sky the
gorgeous flame of summer which is fled!
                                    —Thomas Hood

AUTUMN ALONG DALLAS DIVIDE, OURAY COUNTY

Spring along Dallas Divide, Ouray County

EARLY AUTUMN REFLECTIONS ALONG U.S. HIGHWAY 550, LA PLATA COUNTY

SUMMER ASPENS, ROUTT NATIONAL FOREST

FOLLOWING PAGE: AUTUMN FOLIAGE BELOW PEAKS OF THE UNCOMPAHGRE WILDERNESS

*My words are tied in one
With the great mountains,
With the great rocks,
With the great trees,
In one with my body
And my heart.*
   —**From a Yokut prayer**

PONDEROSA PINES IN THE WET MOUNTAINS BACKDROPPED BY THE SANGRE DE CRISTO RANGE

Gambel oaks, Castle Pines, Douglas County

ASPENS AND WILD ROSES, GUNNISON NATIONAL FOREST

Aspen boles, White River National Forest

Fresh snow along Dallas Divide, Ouray County

FALLEN ASPEN LEAVES ALONG DIVIDE ROAD, UNCOMPAHGRE NATIONAL FOREST

Come said the wind
To the leaves one day,
Come o'er the meadows
And we will play.
Put on your dresses
Scarlet and gold,
For summer is gone
and the days grow cold.
—A children's song, circa 1886

Winter Aspens, White River National Forest

Spring aspens, Routt National Forest

Autumn oaks and ponderosa pines, Castle Pines, Douglas County

In the woods, too, a man casts off his years, as the snake his slough, and at what period so ever of life is always a child.
—Ralph Waldo Emerson

CONIFERS ALONG THE WEST DOLORES RIVER, SAN JUAN NATIONAL FOREST

Spring aspen forest, Grand Mesa National Forest

Grand aspens along Divide Road, Uncompahgre National Forest

following page: Autumn aspens along Divide Road, Uncompahgre National Forest

EARLY AUTUMN SNOWFALL, ROUTT NATIONAL FOREST

Green calm below, blue quietness above.
—John Greenleaf Whittier

SPRING ASPEN BOUQUETS ALONG DIVIDE ROAD, UNCOMPAHGRE NATIONAL FOREST

Spruce-fir forest, Weminuche Wilderness

The greatest wonder is that we can see these trees and not wonder more.
—Ralph Waldo Emerson, from a conversation with John Muir

CONIFERS IN VOLCANIC TUFF, WHEELER GEOLOGIC AREA, LA GARITA WILDERNESS

And this, our life, exempt from public haunt, finds tongues in trees, books in the running brooks, sermons in stones, and good in everything.
—William Shakespeare

Cottonwoods along the Gunnison River, Gunnison County

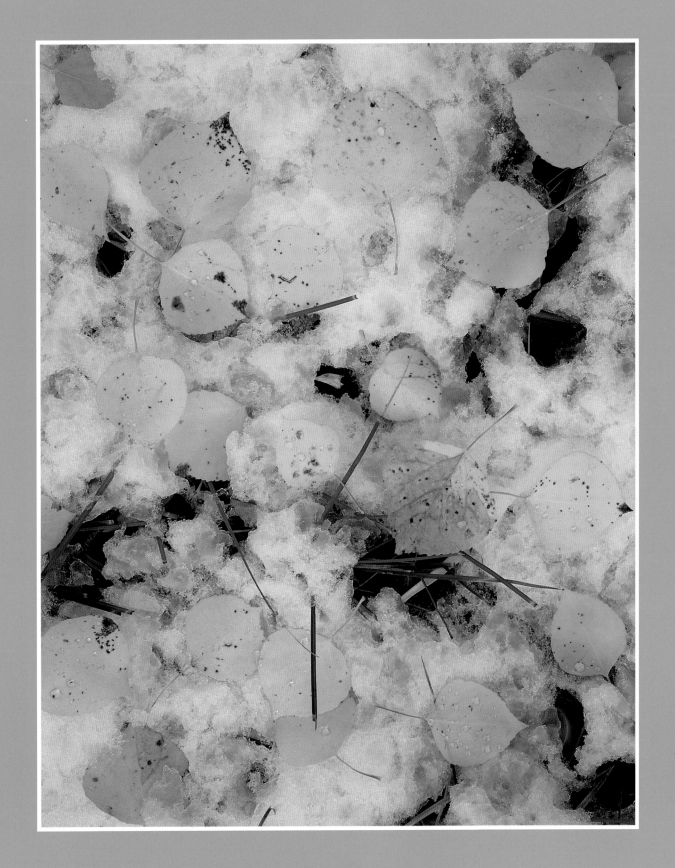

Aspen leaves, Collegiate Peaks Wilderness

The road to Trappers Lake, White River National Forest

Along Lime Creek Road, San Juan National Forest

following page: Spring aspens along the West Dolores River, San Juan National Forest

Old-growth conifers, Mount Zirkel Wilderness

Riverbanks lined with green trees, fragrant grasses: a place not sacred? Where?
—**Zen verse**

EAST CATARACT CREEK, WHITE RIVER NATIONAL FOREST

I went to the woods because I wished to live deliberately, to front only the essential facts of life, and see if I could not learn what it had to teach, and not when I came to die, discover that I had not lived.
—Henry David Thoreau

CROOKED CREEK PASS AREA, WHITE RIVER NATIONAL FOREST

Newly leafed cottonwood, Black Ridge Canyons Wilderness

JOHN FIELDER'S
COLORADO

Visit John Fielder's Colorado in person or on the Web!

See many of the images in this book as framed, fine-art, limited-edition prints at John Fielder's new gallery located in Denver's Cherry Creek Mall, 3000 E. 1st Ave., (303) 744-7979. Also visit **johnfielder.com** to view images from this book and hundreds more, all available online as limited-edition prints in sizes of up to eight feet in width. You can also find John Fielder's complete offering of books and calendars both at the gallery and online.

International Standard Book Number: 1-56579-491-5

Photography copyright: John Fielder, 2003.
All rights reserved.
Text copyright: Steve Smith, 2003. All rights reserved.
Illustrations copyright: Evan Cantor, 2003.
All rights reserved.

Editor: Jenna Samelson Browning
Production Manager: Craig Keyzer

Published by:
Westcliffe Publishers, Inc.
P.O. Box 1261
Englewood CO 80150
westcliffepublishers.com

Printed in China by: C & C Offset Printing, Ltd.

Library of Congress Cataloging-in-Publication Data:
Fielder, John.
    Seeing Colorado's forests for the trees / photography
    by John Fielder ; text by Steve Smith.
        p. cm.
    ISBN 1-56579-491-5
    1. Trees--Colorado. 2. Trees--Colorado--Pictorial
    works. 3. Forest ecology--Colorado.
    I. Smith, Steve, 1951- II. Title.

QK150.F543 2003
582.16'09788--dc21   2003053525

For information about John Fielder books and calendars, as well as Westcliffe titles by other authors and photographers, please contact your local bookstore, call us at 1-800-523-3692, write for our free color catalog, or visit us online at westcliffepublishers.com.